'D' Company
and Black 'Ell
Two Plays by
Miles Malleson

LONDON : HENDERSONS
66 CHARING CROSS ROAD

Printing Statement:

Due to the very old age and scarcity of this book,
many of the pages may be hard to read due to the
blurring of the original text, possible missing pages,
missing text, dark backgrounds and other issues
beyond our control.

Because this is such an important and rare work, we
believe it is best to reproduce this book regardless of
its original condition.

Thank you for your understanding.

Preface

'D' COMPANY was written towards the close of 1914, while I was a private in a Territorial battalion at Malta.

It is, in one sense, real: there is scarcely a sentence in it that I did not hear, or an episode I did not witness.

It is, in another sense, unreal: it is impossible, even for the purposes of realism, to set down here in print the actual language of my barrack-room. The three or four unpleasant words that occurred extraordinarily often and in the queerest series of combinations and connections, not only created a certain atmosphere of ugliness that would be necessary for any really true picture of life then, but also supplied a sort of lilt to the conversation that cannot be reproduced without them.

I should like to add here that while those months were, I think, the unhappiest I have lived through, I have the very liveliest memories of much from my companions and friends of 'D' Company, for which I feel I can never be sufficiently grateful.

Some slight foot trouble was responsible for my

being invalided home and out of the Army. That was in January, 1915.

Since then my view of this colossal catastrophe of the war has changed.

'Black 'Ell' has been just recently written.

M. M.

London, September, 1916.

'D' Company

'D' COMPANY

CHARACTERS

PRIVATE ALF TIBBUTT.

PRIVATE TILLEY.

PRIVATE JIM PENLEY.

PRIVATE DENNIS GARSIDE.

CORPORAL CHARLES JOYNER.

AN ORDERLY CORPORAL.

All of 'D' Company in a Territorial Battalion.

SCENE: *A Barrack Room.*

TIME: *October* 1914.

The scene is a men's mess-room in barracks at Malta, in which is stationed an English Territorial regiment, mobilised now and proud of being on the same terms as the regulars ; but, having only been soldiers in grim earnest for a short while (the Great War is now in its third month), they are all very much English civilians under their khaki uniforms.

Directly facing the audience are five small folding iron bedsteads, with mattresses, rugs, and coarse white sheets neatly and uniformly folded upon them. Over the beds are racks upon which the men keep their 'equipment' (belt and shoulder-straps, bayonet-carrier, haversack, water-bottle, mess-tin, entrenching-tool, overcoat, and ammunition pouches—quite a good load on a march), and behind each bed a wooden rest for the rifle. Immediately in front of each bed is a black wooden box in which each man keeps his personal belongings.

About the middle of the stage is a wooden table and two forms at which the men feed. Big windows are in the wall behind the beds—i.e., the wall facing the audience —and the door is in this wall. A wooden cupboard is on one of the side walls.

When the curtain rises, PRIVATE TILLEY *is already in bed—a little, round, stubby man with a stubby moustache. Two months ago he delivered coals. Now his mouth is open and he snores.*

On the bed next to him sits ALF—*a thorough young blackguard; perhaps twenty-two, but he is under-grown and doesn't look it. A van-boy somewhere in the City. Cockney from top to toe. He is cleaning his rifle.*

A bugle in the distance sounds the 'Last Post.'

THE ORDERLY CORPORAL *passes the window outside and puts his head in.*

THE ORDERLY CORPORAL'S HEAD.   Where's the Corporal in charge of this room?

ALF.   [*Shortly.*]   Ain't in yet.

O. C.'S HEAD.   Where is 'e?

ALF.   Dunno.   The Company's on a route march. I'm mess orderly terday.

> [*That as an explanation of his presence in the room; the* ORDERLY CORPORAL'S *eye lights on the snoring* TILLEY.

O. C.'S HEAD. Wot's 'e doin'?

ALF. Sleepin'!!!

O. C.'S HEAD. Wot for?

ALF. Jus' come off guard.

[JIM, *a van-boy friend of* ALF'S, *but younger, fresher, and more boyish-looking, comes into the room.*

O. C.'S HEAD. 'Ullo! Company come back?

JIM. Yus.

O. C.'S HEAD. 'Last Post' gorn. Lights out in 'arf an 'our.

[*The* HEAD *is withdrawn and passes on.* JIM *has come from a long march. Crossing straight to his bed, he takes his full equipment from his shoulders; his rifle goes into its stand. Then crossing to the cupboard, he takes a half-loaf of bread from it. At this point* ALF *begins to take a lively interest in him.* ALF *and* JIM *are 'mates'—had been, behind their vans in Far- ringdon Street — so they can quarrel to their hearts' content. Here a diversion :—Among a great class, differences of opinion, almost continual, invariably mean a quarrel; and a 'quarrel' in- variably means raised voices. That is how* ALF *and* JIM *'quarrelled.' They merely contradicted one another, getting louder and louder until nature asserted herself and they could get no louder. Then they stopped until one or the other said something, and they began all over again. Unknowing that* ALF *had ceased the rifle-cleaning and was watching him with eagle eyes,* JIM *takes the half-loaf from the cupboard.* ALF *rises, crosses to him, and the 'difference of opinion' begins—sudden, staccato, and 'sempre crescendo.'*

ALF. 'Ere, is that the only one there?

JIM. Yus.

ALF. It's mine, then.

JIM. I know it ain't, then.

ALF. I know it is.

JIM. I know it ain't.

ALF. [*His face close to* JIM'S, *and an arm outstretched to drive home his accusation.*] Didn't you sit at that there table at dinner-time an' I save mine an' you et all yourn?

JIM. I never.

ALF. I saw yer.

JIM. You never.

ALF. I tell yer I saw yer.

JIM. I tell yer you never.

> [*By that time they can get no louder, so there is a tiny space of silence, broken suddenly by a terrific burst of snoring from* TILLEY. *The two boys turn to the bed. Another burst from the open-mouthed sleeper, and their difference is forgotten.* JIM *throws the half-loaf a high toss, so that it drops nicely on the bulge under the rugs that is* TILLEY'S *stomach.* TILLEY *stirs, grunts, and mutters.*

TILLEY. Aw'ri'—aw'ri'—aw'ri'! I'll get up. Make us a cup—er—tea—'*ot*, ol' girl; make it '*ot*, you know. Aw'ri'—I'll get up.

ALF [*Touched.*] Blimee! 'E thinks 'e's at 'ome. Let the pore blighter be. I wish I was 'im. Battersea—not 'arf!

> [JIM *picks up the half-loaf from where it rests.*

ALF. [*With a ferocity so sudden that* JIM *obeys.*] '*Ere, give that 'ere;* an' I shan't give yer none neether.

If you 'adn't tried to pinch mine I'd 'ave given you arf ; now you can jolly well go wivvout—see ?

> [JIM'S *answer is disconcerting. In a dignified silence he walks over to his box at the foot of his bed and takes out a half-loaf of bread. He sits on his box and begins to enjoy it. ALF returns his to the cupboard. The vicious slam with which it goes in and with which the door is closed upon it marks a palpable hit to* JIM. THE CORPORAL *in charge of the room enters. He is perhaps fifty years old, though he made the recruiting-sergeant write him down forty-four and eleven months. In London he mends roads. A curious blend of the navvy and the ex-soldier—and one of nature's gentlemen, with a strong open-air refinement about him. He, too, has come off the march. He goes to his bed.*

CORPORAL. [*As he lifts his equipment off his shoulders, and stretches after the load is removed.*] Ten miles, my lads ; not bad for an old 'un. I can teach you youngsters a bit about soljering yet. [*Then he goes to the cupboard and takes out the half-loaf of bread.*] Makes a man 'ungry this do. Lucky I saved my bit er rooty [*bread*].

> [ALF *avoids* JIM'S *eye ! The* CORPORAL, *coming down to the table, gathers the two boys to him.*

CORPORAL. 'Ere, 'ere, my lads ; come 'ere, I got something to tell yer. Yer know *'im ?* [*He indicates an empty bed.*]

JIM. Oo ?

CORPORAL. *'Im.*

ALF. [*To* JIM.] The one wot lies there—the young bloke wot never says nuffink.

JIM. O, '*im!* Yus.

CORPORAL. [*Getting big with mystery.*] Yus! And you've got to mind wot yer says to '*im*, too.

JIM. Go on !

[*Meaning 'You don't say so' or 'Fancy that.'*]

CORPORAL. Yus, you 'ave! I've rumbled 'im all right, I 'ave. Shall I tell you wot 'e is ?

JIM. [*Thinking himself brilliant.*] Go on! 'E ain't a German spy ?

CORPORAL. German spy yerself! 'E's a *gentleman* —that's wot 'e is. Aye, and a proper one, too. I'm only a navvy, I am ... but I knows. 'E's stacks above us, 'e his. 'E's got money, 'e 'as. Bags ... a ninkum, an' a proper 'ouse and edjucation—Cambridge College —*I* knows.

JIM. Go on!

CORPORAL. Yus.

TILLEY. [*From his bed with a suddenness unexpected from an apparent sleeper.*] Ju think I didn't know *that?* You think you knows everythink, you do. I guess I knows a sight more abut gentlemen than you do any day. Navvy! I take coals to their 'ouses every day, I do.

JIM. Blimee—'e ain't arf quiet, is 'e ?

ALF. Don't gentlemen never say nuffink ?

CORPORAL. Garn !—ju s'pose 'e'd want ter talk to *you ?* You're a nignorant lot, you are.

[*This is a signal for another ' difference.'*]

TILLEY. Hignorant! We knows as much as you do any day.

CORPORAL. You! Wot ju know about soljering. You don't know nuffink. Twenty-seven years' service —with the Reg'lars, mind you, none o' yer Terr-i-tor-ials [*a fine contempt in that.*] Twen .. ty-seven years' service —that's me. You! Ten drills a year!

ALF. If you'd 'ad to walk annuver mile—it 'ud 'av killed yer—*grandfavver.*

CORPORAL. Grandfather!... why they ever took you away from yer mother I don't know ... grandfather. Ho!... I can walk as far as you can any day.

ALF. I know yer can't.

CORPORAL. I know I can.

ALF. I know yer can't, then.

[*That is not as loud as he can go, and he would probably have gone one better, but the discussed occupant of the empty bed* ENTERS, *and rather because they have been discussing him a sudden, almost uncomfortable, silence ensues.* DENNIS GARSIDE *is a young man of twenty-two—fresh from Cambridge. Slightly but well built; quiet in manner. He is not particularly shy, and is by no means a Eugene Marchbanks, but there is much of the sensitiveness of the artist about him. He goes to his bed and unloads himself of his equipment. The group disperse, throwing themselves on their several beds. Before putting his rifle in his rack,* DENNIS *starts to clean it.*

CORPORAL. That's aw' right, my lad. You put that by. *I'll* clean that for yer in the mornin'!

[DENNIS *hesitates.*

CORPORAL. Got any cleanin' kit, 'ave yer? Brushes and things?

DENNIS. In my box.

CORPORAL. Well, you don't need to worry about no cleanin'—buttons, boots, rifle—nuffink... I'll see about that for yer—don't you worry.

DENNIS. [*As he puts up his rifle.*] Well... Thanks awfully.   [*The newness of the expression tickles* ALF.

ALF. ' Thanks aw'fly.'

CORPORAL. [*Like a cartload of his own bricks.*] *Stoppit*... Young Alf—j' 'ear ?—Stoppit...

DENNIS. [*Ignoring the interruption.*] It's kind of you—but really I can do it quite well for myself...

CORPORAL. That's aw' right... You don't need to worry... I've rumbled *you*, I 'ave

DENNIS. I beg your pardon ?

CORPORAL. I've *rumbled* yer, all right. 'Ere. [*He nods to* DENNIS *to come close to his bed, and addresses him in a hoarse whisper.*] You're not used ter this sort of thing, are yer ?

DENNIS. Well, no... not exactly.

CORPORAL. [*With a wise nod.*] You don't need ter worry. *I'll* see yer thro' aw' right. See ? There ain't much I don't know about soljering. I come out of the Reg'lar Army, I do. Twenty-seven years' service... This lot ! Territorials or whatever they call theirselves— they don't know NUFFINK !

ALF. [*Addressing the air.*] GRANDFAVVER.

CORPORAL. Don't you listen to 'em... HIGNORANCE —that's wot it is... Just HIGNORANCE... What's yer name, boy ?

DENNIS. Garside.

CORPORAL. Yer other ?

DENNIS. Oh... Dennis.

CORPORAL. Dennis... Charlie's mine. You call me Charlie.

ALF. Call 'im grandfavver... that's wot 'e is.

CORPORAL. [*To himself.*] Ten drills a year. Soljers !!! ... Dennis. You 'ave a lie-down, boy, like us.

[DENNIS *settles himself to a welcome rest after the ten-mile march. The others have now all pulled their folding bedsteads out to their full length, and are stretched upon them.*

JIM. 'Ere, Alf.

ALF. 'Ullo!

JIM. Juno wot I 'eard?

ALF. Wot?

JIM. We're goin' to the Front. 15th next monf.

ALF. Front! I know we ain't, then.

JIM. I know we are! An' I tell yer 'ow I knows. 'Cos that bloke with red 'air an' a narsty neck in E Company 'e told Jack their Captain tell them ... 'e did —on p'rade—a fact ... The Front ... Next monf.

ALF. You're a liar. An' I tell yer why ... We're goin' ter Africa.

TILLEY. Africa. I don't fink.

ALF. Yus we are then. There's a rebellion. Bores. I know fer a fact, 'cos my chum knows a Nofficer's servant, and Kernel's servant says 'e 'eard the Kernel say so. There you are. The Kernel's own lips. You can't get over that.

CORPORAL. Africa. Hignorance. You won't see no Hafrica. *An'* you won't see no Front. Don't *you* worry yer guts. But I'll tell you wot you *will* see, and that jolly quick too—'OME. That's you—'OME. You're only 'ere to relieve the Reg'lars. 'Ow long ju think the war'll last? ... why, they kills thousands of Germans every day—every *hour* almost.

ALF. They've got cholera, ain't they?

CORPORAL. *'Corse* they 'ave, *an'* typhoid—*an'* enteric.

JIM. It says in the paper they're starvin'—eatin' grass.

B

CORPORAL. *'Corse* they are. Boys an' old men, that's all they've got left now.

ALF. You ought ter bin a German, grandfavver. You might 'er bin some use ter them.

CORPORAL. *You* at the Front. It'll be all over long afore you knows which end of a rifle the bullet comes out of!

TILLEY. Wot you join us for? Pity you didn't go back to yer own lot. Always growsin'!

CORPORAL. Ah! that *would* 'ave been soljering, that would. They wouldn't 'ave me. I'm a nold man, I am. Fifty, tho' I don't look it. Forty-four and eleven months, that's wot this lot's got me down. Though there's as much soljering left in me as there is in fifty 'er you any day. I'm a navvy, I am. With a nold woman and five kids. That's why I come out. I see the Red Lamp up ahead—danger. Me out 'er work—and them to feed. Now she's gettin' a tidy bit for me bein' 'ere—and I'm not at 'ome eatin'... see? They're aw' right, they are. That's why I come out.

ALF. They jus' chucked us out 'ere, didn't they, Jim? Get sacked out of our jobs, or come 'ere and 'ave 'em kept.

JIM. Yus. [*Then to* DENNIS.] Weren't there no jobs goin' in your line, so you 'ad to come?

DENNIS. Me? Oh, well, yes... No... I don't know... I suppose I *needn't* have come?

TILLEY. Wot's your line, mister?

DENNIS. I don't know...

ALF. Coo blimee!

DENNIS. I mean, I'm just at home.

CORPORAL. Hignorance. The Hignorantest lot I ever see.

ALF. Didn't you 'ave to leave no job?

DENNIS. No.

ALF. Didn't you 'ave to work for a livin'?

DENNIS. No.

ALF. Coo... split me... why ju come then?

DENNIS. [*A trifle haltingly.*] I dunno. Suppose one felt one ought to *do* something, you know... one's country... they wouldn't have me in Kitchener's army ... my eyes... so I joined you.

> [*This is received in a solemn silence, broken by the* ORDERLY CORPORAL'S *head at the window.*

O. CORPORAL. Private Tibbutt.

ALF. That's me.

O. CORPORAL. Paper for you and two letters.

> [*That brings them all off their beds as if the latter had suddenly become red-hot.*

ALF.			Letters?
TILLEY.	}	*Together.* {	Any for me?
CORPORAL.			'Ere, got one for Joyner?
JIM.			Letters? Give us one...

O. CORPORAL. [*Quieting the storm.*] No, there ain't none for nobody, only Tibbutt. There's some more down in the orderly room — unsorted — may be up to-night — probably to-morrer... 'Oo's in charge 'ere?

CORPORAL IN CHARGE. Me.

O. CORPORAL. Last post gorn.

C. IN C. Right, Corporal. I'll see 'em in bed.

O. CORPORAL. 'Eard the latest?

TILLEY. Wot's that, then?

O. CORPORAL. The Front... us... month after next ... straight across to Mah-sales.

ALF. Front, eh? Blimee!

O. CORPORAL. That's right. Sergeant-Major's just told us—down in the Orderly-room. 'E knows.

[O. CORPORAL *withdraws his head again and is gone.*

JIM. The Front, eh? Coo blimee! that's broke it.

[ALF *has pocketed his two letters, but is seated at the table with his newspaper spread before him.* JIM *looks over his shoulder.*

JIM. The *Mirror*—it's took ten days comin'... Coo—look! Them's Germans—the barsterds! Never mind the wa-er. 'Oo beat—Chelsea or the Arsenal?

ALF. Chelsea, 'corse; they'd beat the Arsenal any day.

JIM. I know they wouldn't.

ALF. I know they would.

JIM. I know they wouldn't, then.

ALF. [*Commencing his loudest and therefore last retort.*] I tell yer I knows...

[*And then a dead silence. His eye has caught something in the paper before him. The silence is so sudden that it is noticeable... all eyes turn to him.*

ALF. [*After a moment—a stifled, heart-broken cry.*] Gaw blimee!

JIM. Wot's up, mate?

[ALF *points to a passage in the paper.* JIM *looks. The rest wait — a questioning silence.* JIM *answers it.*

JIM. It's them lists.

CORPORAL. Casualties?

JIM. Yus.

TILLEY. 'Oo?

JIM. 'Is young bruvver.

ALF. [*His voice strange and subdued.*] Read it, Jim boy. Wot's it say after 'is name?

JIM. 'Private Thomas Tibbutt, 2nd East Surrey Rifles. Shot in the ad ... ad ... ab ... do ... men ...'

TILLEY. That means stummerk, that does.

JIM. Yus. 'Shot in the ad ... ab ... do ... men, died of wounds.'

[*Another short silence, full of unexpressed compassion. A little gulping sound comes from* ALF. *With a terrific sniff, he rises from the table and goes to his rifle. Taking it from his rack, he begins a vigorous and totally unnecessary cleaning of it.*

CORPORAL. [*Feeling that something ought to be said and that he is the one to say it.*] I'm sorry, boy; that's bad, that is.

ALF. 'E was the only one bar me. We was mates, we was. [*A second terrific rubbing of an already spotless barrel; then*] Coo blimee! Young Tom ... young Tom. 'E can't be dead ... you can't seem ter think. I shan't never see 'im no more.

[*He abandons his rifle and sits on his bed, broken.*

JIM. [*Going to his box and taking something out of it.*] 'Ere, boy—'ave something to eat.

[*He offers the remains of his secreted half-loaf;* ALF *shakes his head.*

CORPORAL. Best leave 'im alone for a bit. I knows wot it is, I do. Lost a kid before now. Quarter of an hour before lights out, boys. 'Oo's for a bit of a smoke?

[*He begins to fill a pipe and saunters uneasily from the room.* TILLEY, *still in bed, settles himself to sleep again.* JIM *follows the* CORPORAL *from the room.*

ALF. [*His voice stopping* DENNIS, *who is also following, in the doorway.*] 'Ere, Mister!

DENNIS. Yes?

ALF. 'Ere... if it ain't a liberty, would you mind doin' something fer me?

DENNIS. Rather, of course, anything.

ALF. These 'ere letters (*he pulls them from his pocket*). I ain't much of a 'and at readin'. Not proper. I knows 'oo they're from. One's from my old muvver and one from my wife.'

DENNIS. (*Surprise getting the better of him.*) Are you married?

ALF. Yus. Two kids. Not 'arf fine 'uns neether. (*He breaks the seals.*) Would you tell me wot's in 'em? Read 'em out like... if it's not a liberty. Some'ow I thought you wouldn't mind. The writing ain't much— but I expect you'll be able to say wot they're abaht.'

[DENNIS *takes them. After a glance round at* TILLEY, *who is apparently asleep again, they shift along the table as far from him as possible, and* DENNIS *begins to read, in a low voice. The simplicity with which he reads covers anything in them that might otherwise seem ridiculous, and rather emphasises the pity of them.*

DENNIS. This one?

ALF. Yus. That's from my wife, that is.

DENNIS (*reading*). '137B Paradise Gardens, Battersea.'

ALF. That's right. That's where I lives.

DENNIS. 'Oh, my dear Alf, I sit down to write you a few lines hoping you are quite well as this letter leaves me. Oh, my dear Alf, I have got bad news to tell you. But you must be brave and not think about it too much. Alf, Tom has been killed at the front. It is terrible. Your mother heard it yesterday. Tom's girl come round here last night. I tried to say something to her, but it don't seem no good. She cried something dreadful.

Dear Alf, I do miss you terrible. I do pray you may come back to me safe. Little Alf is fine, but Baby has a cold. I am doing all right on the money I gets for you. I send you four packets of woodbines because I knows you like them, but I can't afford no more. Dear Alf, I am so looking forward to you coming home. I must close now. A big kiss from little Alf and Baby and me. God bless you, my dear Alf.—Ever your loving wife, LOO.'

> [*There is a pause. ALF* can only nod, and has to wipe the back of his hand across his nose and sniff.

ALF. Thank yer... look at them crosses. They're kisses, they are. Wot's it say under 'em?

DENNIS. 'From little Alf. From Baby. From me.'

ALF. That one from 'er?

DENNIS. Yes.

ALF. Coo! That's the biggest, that is ... now the other one, please ... this is from my muvver, this is.

DENNIS (*reading*). 'King Edward VII. Mansions, 304 H Block, Hammersmith.'

ALF. That's where she lives.

DENNIS. 'My dear Alf,—I have terrible bad news to tell you. Yesterday they come and tell me Tom had been killed.

'Dear Alf, I do not know how to bear it. He was hurt something horrible in the stomach, and didn't die for two days afterwards. They tried not to tell me that part, but I knows because old Mrs. Hayes had a letter from a pal of Tom in his regiment.

'Oh, dear Alf, do not go to the Front. If you have any love for me do not go. They says in the papers here mothers ought to be proud to give their sons, but

them what writes that ain't mothers with sons to give.
Alf, I have given one and I have only you left.

'Oh, Alf, come home safe to me. I prays to God all
day that you may—but, Alf, don't go if yer can help it.
I must close now. I can only think of my Tom and
you all the time sitting here.

'Good-bye, and God keep you safe.—Your ever loving
MOTHER.

'P.S.—Loo come round last night,after she heard about
Tom. Baby has a cold, but little Alf is all right!'

[*Another pause.*

ALF. That ain't 'arf a letter to get from yer muvver,
is it? Gives a feller the fair 'ump—proper, it do. [*Which
is, if you come to think of it, quite as picturesque as saying
one has a bleeding heart.*]... Mister, would you write an
answer for me... If I tells yer wot to say?

DENNIS. Of course... now?

ALF. Yus—if yer don't mind.

DENNIS. Rather.

[*He takes a writing pad, &c., from the box at the
foot of his bed and brings them to the table. He
begins writing.*

ALF. Wot ju puttin'?

DENNIS. Only the address of the barracks. What's
your number?

ALF. Number twenty-two twenty-seven D Company.

DENNIS. Right (*and he waits, pen in hand*). You
must tell me what to put.

ALF. I'm no 'and at letters. Wot 'ud *you* put, if you
was me?

DENNIS. Just say anything you like; I'll write it down.

ALF. [*After vain searching for expression.*] It don't
seem no good sayin' nuffink. A feller can't say wot 'e

feels. It's all—*you* know—mixed up inside. Nuffink I say won't bring young Tom back, will it ?

DENNIS. No.

ALF. ... 'My dear Loo.' [*Then another pause. Alf goes off at a tangent.*] Mister, are you married ?

DENNIS. No.

ALF. You got a girl, ain't yer ?

DENNIS. Yes.

ALF. Ju write all that wot you writes to 'er ?

DENNIS. Some of it.

ALF. I bet you don't 'arf write letters to 'er neether. [*He points to two or three pages of foolscap in the writing pad.*] Is them to 'er ?

DENNIS. Yes.

ALF. Coo. I wouldn't 'arf like to know what you says to 'er. I s'pose you wouldn't read me a bit—would yer? I shouldn't 'arf like to 'ear. It might give me an idea-like for mine—p'raps.

    [DENNIS *hesitates—he handles his unfinished letter*
           —he smiles with the quaintness of the idea.

DENNIS. Would you like to hear ?

ALF. Not 'arf.

DENNIS. I'll read it if you like.

ALF. You're a proper toff, you are.

    [DENNIS *has a glance at* TILLEY—*eyes closed, mouth*
        open, so he begins reading with the same simple
        directness with which he read the others ; without
        the least effort after dramatic effect.

DENNIS. ' "Child of the lonely heart"—that's from Edward Carpenter ; I have his book here, for which may he be eternally blessed—I would not dare call you that for my sake except that you sign yourself with that adjective.

'Oh, my dear, my dear; here I sit, pen in hand, just overflowing with the need of you, and unable to find words to tell you about it. My comfort is that there is no need—you know. You ask for news of our life here. How shall I begin? It is difficult. Chiefly because I want to tell you about your eyes and your hair—the stray bits of it that wave about your forehead—and your voice and your laugh—'

ALF. [*Sotto voce.*] Coo blimee!

DENNIS. '— and our good-bye. Oh, my dear, on the platform, before all the people! D'you know I was wondering whether you would. Such a quick, tiny one —but it will go on for ever. There are some moments in our lives when the world seems to stop still and they get photographed—through the ages that moment will be part of my mental scenery as long as I have a mind.

'Oh, you, you, you. I am all You at the moment, and if I take the line of least resistance and put pen to paper, out you come like water from a tap. However, I am a soldier now—so Discipline!

'Attention! Our life here: From 5 in the morning till 5 at night, learning how to avoid getting a piece of red-hot lead into oneself, and how best to put it into somebody else.'

ALF. Crikee!

DENNIS 'We are off the parade-ground now, and spend all day in the open, skirmishing, with occasional welcome changes of duty. Two nights ago I was on coast defence. It was a strange experience—standing alone at 2 o'clock in the morning, only the sound of the sea in one's ears, rifle in hand, on guard over a few "mates" asleep under the shelter of some rocks. (The mates asleep, not me.)

' The first time one challenges a dark moving figure is a real sensation.

' This is a land of theatrical effects. "The living blue breathless miracle, the sky" (Carpenter) changes in a moment to a pale transparent grey and the grey to a limitless star-strewn blackness, for all the world as if it were being worked on a switchboard—and the moon climbs up the sky as if it were being pulled with ropes and pulleys by a crowd of sweating angels, coats off and braces showing—and its light floods on to the Mediterranean like a back-cloth of Sir Herbert Tree's. And after hours of guard, to see the dawn break over the sea in a ridiculous hurry in wildly unnatural colours and sudden broad dazzling daylight, and a march back to barracks to sleep like a log on one's mattress till a bugle breaks into one's experience, and up and doing something else.

' Rumours are thick as to our future movements.

' I will confess to you, my dear (if confession it is), that I am not one of the many who are burning with an eagerness to get into the firing line. I think, if I aimed at a German officer, the obvious symbol of Prussian Militarism, I should be sure to miss him and hit a private who would probably be a Social Democrat with many an idea in common with me, or a musician who has felt as I have over the passion of Wagner, or a man who simply loathes fighting as much as I do, and has as many friends behind him in his land as I in mine.

'And if I knew he loved one of them as I do—may the Lord Kitchener forgive me—I think I should aim to miss—which, incidentally, wouldn't make him any the safer from my bullet. All of which is possibly very foolish.

'We are fighting for an idea. Democracy *versus* Militarism, that " mighty long-delaying vagrant stream" (Carpenter again—God bless him), and we must allow no barren rock to stop its course. But life as a private isn't all glory—it's often very ugly. " The vices of men and boys,' as Kipling says somewhere about young soldiers. My companions . . .'

[*And* DENNIS *comes to a sudden stop.*

ALF. Go on, mister, read it all.

[*But* DENNIS *quite evidently doesn't. He picks up the thread some lines on.*

DENNIS. 'And among these strange surroundings I sometimes have to remember very hard about " The Rights of Little Nations and the Sacredness of Treaties" and Asquith, and the Houses of Parliament—rising tall and beautiful against the night sky, as I saw them that memorable night when we declared war. No more now. If I write another word it would be about you. Besides, I have got to be on parade in a minute, and I don't think my buttons are clean enough for our lieutenant. He is as fresh from Cambridge as I am—except that he comes from Oxford! But, oh, the great gulf that our uniforms make between us. You should hear my de-ferential " Sir " and see his haughty look—which is food for thought. *Au revoir.'* . . . That's all I've written yet.

ALF. I reckon that ain't 'arf a letter. Wot's that last word ?

DENNIS. *Au revoir.*

ALF. Is that your name then ? Wot she calls yer, I mean ?

DENNIS. No, that's French.

ALF. Oh! Anyhow, it ain't 'arf a letter. Fine. She must be a One. 'Ave you been goin' out wiv 'er long ?

DENNIS. Yes, fairly.

ALF. Now I must do mine. Let's see—'ow ju start yourn?

DENNIS. 'Child of the lonely heart.'

ALF. Yus. That wouldn't 'ardly do fer my ol' woman. She'd think I was sprucin' 'er.

THE CORPORAL *and* JIM *re-enter.*

CORPORAL. Come on now, boys. Kip—come on. Kip afore lights out.

[*To 'kip' means approximately to get comfortable and go to sleep. The men begin preparing for the night —making their beds, taking their boots and coats off. All of a sudden, loud and clear goes a bugle-call; the effect is startling and instantaneous.*

JIM. [*A wild yell.*] Letters! [*Then, with one voice, the cry goes up,* 'Letters.' *Other men in other rooms can be heard shouting and cheering.*

JIM. [*Singing the well-known words that 'Tommy' has fitted to the tune of the call.*] 'Letters from Lousie Loo, boys; letters from Lousie Loo.' (!)

[*His head out of the window.*] There goes the Orderly Corporal down to the Orderly-room. He'll be up with 'em in a moment. [*He is tremendously excited.*] 'Ere I say, Alf; it's right abut the Front—as soon as we're ready.

TILLEY. 'Ow ju know, then?

JIM. A' officer tell us. It's all round—certain. The Front when we're ready.

CORPORAL. 'When you're ready.' Yus! When!!

ALF. [*His mother's letter in his hand.*] We got to go, then. The letter wot I 'ad from my muvver. It's enough to break a feller's 'eart—it is. [*His letters have, indeed, for a time 'taken the 'eart out of 'im,' as his pals would put it.*] If I goes, I'll follow young Tom. I knows that. Fancy not seein' my kids again ... Little Alf, 'e'll grow up fine ... The missus sent me some cigarettes ... she's a good 'un. [*Then, as if apologising,*] The letter from my muvver fair give me the proper 'ump.

TILLEY. Aye, that's it. It comes 'ard when you've got a 'ome—an' a wife—and children. Sometimes I get thinkin'. Damn the war, I says. My 'ome—wot's to 'appen if I clicks. [*'To click' means to find oneself fixed for something one can't get out of. He means, of course, if he gets killed.*] It's aw' right for them wot 'as no one dependin' on 'em.

DENNIS. [*The reading of his letters has brought him rather more out of himself than usual.*] People say that, but they don't know. After all, life has given you something. You've had a home of your own and a wife, and seen your own children—your very own. With us it's all to come. We've only looked into a girl's eyes and seen the promise of such wonderful things. [*And in his low voice are all the yearnings of the sleepless nights he has spent since he left England. His tone changes.*] But what's the use of talking? What's to come's to come—and that's all about it ... So what's the use of worrying?

CORPORAL. [*Approving.*] That's it, lad. That's the soljer ... Ready to make the best of it, and we'll clear every bloody German off the face of the earth—they won't never see *their* 'omes again.

TILLEY. *An'* serve 'em right—barsterds!

ALF. Pore blighters.

[*Enter the* ORDERLY CORPORAL *with a bundle of letters and papers. Immediately they are round*

him, leaping like savages round a ritualistic fire,
buzzing like bees round a honey-pot.

O. CORPORAL. [*Reading names on the envelope of his*
bundle.] Private Tilley.

TILLEY. 'Ere. [*He gets a letter.*

O. CORPORAL. Private Thomas, Private Oakley,
Private Stubbs, Private Penley.

JIM. 'Ere. [*He gets a letter.*

O. CORPORAL. Private Penley. [*He gets another.*]
Corporal Harding, Private Pearce, Corporal Joyner.

C. IN C. Me. [*He gets a letter.*

O. CORPORAL. Private Tibbutt.

[ALF *is the only one taking little interest.*

JIM. 'Ere, Alf; 'ere's one for you.

O. CORPORAL. Come on! Hurry yerself! Take
it ... wot's the matter wiv yer?

JIM. 'Is young bruvver's bin rubbed out, Corporal—
at the Front.

O. CORPORAL. Oh! 'ere, lad—'ere's a letter.

ALF. [*Taking it.*] Thank yer.

O. CORPORAL. Private Garside.

DENNIS. Here, Corporal. [*He gets a letter.*

O. CORPORAL. There's a lot for yer. Private Garside—Garside—Garside ... [DENNIS *gathers them to*
himself.] That's the lot ... Good-night!

OMNES. G—night, Corporal.

[*They all sit on their beds, drinking in their letters*
like a thirsty soldier at a pot of beer. Of a sudden
all the lights go out. From the blackness comes a
howl of execration. Howl after howl—and on
this the Curtain slides down.

THE END.

Black 'Ell

BLACK 'ELL

About nine o'clock on an August morning in 1916,
MR. AND MRS. GOULD *are having breakfast. They
have been happily married some twenty-five years. Their
income is about a thousand a year, and there is nothing to
differentiate their dining-room—or their whole house, for
that matter—from other dining-rooms and houses of the
same class.*

MR. GOULD *is reading a daily paper propped up against
something on the table. Presently he drains his large
coffee-cup and pushes it across to his wife. She re-fills it,
carries it round to him, and returns to her place. The
breakfast continues. He finishes the bacon and eggs on his
plate. She has been watching, and asks him if he will
have any more. She does that by a little noise—a little
upward inflection of inquiry and affection.' (The affection
is unconscious and unobtrusive—the result of twenty-five
years and about nine thousand breakfasts together.)*

*The little noise catches his attention from his paper. He
eyes his own empty plate ; he eyes the inviting egg on the
dish in front of her, and grunts. A little downward
inflection of assent. He gets his second helping and the
breakfast continues in silence.*

*   *   *   *   *

*Then, quite suddenly, crashing into the silence, a loud
double-knock at the front door, followed by a violent ring-
ing. It is as if they had both been hit unexpectedly.*

MRS. GOULD. A telegram!

MR. GOULD. Sounds like it.

[*Their eyes meet in anxiety. She rises in the grip of fear.*

MRS. GOULD. Oh, Fred, d'you think it's ... can it be *that*, at last? Have you looked ... the casualty page?

MR. GOULD. Yes, yes, of course I've looked. I always look first thing ... you know that as well as I do.

MRS. GOULD. It wouldn't be there ... not till to-morrow. They always send from the War Office first ... by telegram.

MR. GOULD. [*Trying to quiet her in a voice that trembles with anxiety.*] Now, mother, mother, we go all through this every time a simple telegram comes to the house.

MRS. GOULD. [*Back in her seat, too frightened to do anything but just sit there and wait.*] It's about *him*, I feel ... I know it's about him.

MR. GOULD. Don't be silly. [*He goes up to the window.*] There's the boy ... it's a telegram all right ... Why doesn't Ethel answer the door? ... Oh, there, she's taken it in. [*He comes away from the window. Again their eyes meet.*] Now, mother, there's no need to be anxious ... not the slightest reason to get frightened ... not the slightest. [*With a poor attempt at a laugh to fill in the wait.*] What a fuss about a telegram! [*The wait lengthens.*] ... Where *is* Ethel? ... I wish the devil people would use the telephone.

[*And even as he eyes it reproachfully, the thing rings. It startles them both.*

MR. GOULD. [*Ungratefully.*] Damn it!... [*Attending to it.*] Yes? Hullo!... What's the matter?... What is it?

ETHEL, *the maid, enters.*

ETHEL. A telegram, sir.

[MR. GOULD *doesn't want his wife to open it, but he is attached to the telephone.*

MR. GOULD. [*Holding out his spare hand for it.*] Here, give it to me.

[ETHEL *gives it to him and stands waiting. He continues into the telephone.*]

Yes?... I can't hear... Who are you?

MRS. GOULD. [*Tortured by the delay.*] Oh, Fred... Please... finish talking... and open it.

MR. GOULD. Don't be silly, dear. [*Then hastily to the telephone.*] No, no, nothing. No. I wasn't talking to you... Oh... yes... very well, come round. [*He rings off.*] It's that Willis girl. I never can hear a word she says... she seemed very excited about something... said she wanted to come round.

MRS. GOULD. It may be about him. Some news in the papers we haven't seen. Please... please... tell me what's in it.

MR. GOULD. Nothing to do with the boy at all, you bet your life... somebody wants to meet me at the club.

[*His hands are trembling and he is having some difficulty in opening it. It comes out upside down. At last he gets it right and looks at it; but his eyes aren't so good as he always thinks they are.*

Where are my spectacles?

MRS. GOULD. Oh, Fred!

MR. GOULD. Mother, don't be silly. Ethel, where are my spectacles?... I had 'em.

> [*He gropes on the table. It is* ETHEL *that finds them. Adjusting them, he reads the message and hands the telegram to his wife.*

MRS. GOULD. Oh, my dear... father... my dear...

> [*The tears in her voice overwhelm her words.*

MR. GOULD. There, there, there... mother... now quiet.

MRS GOULD. Yes.

> [ETHEL *has not left the room; she is standing awkwardly, but unable to go, by the door.*

MR. GOULD. Ethel, Master Harold is in England again... it's from him... he's home on leave... he'll be back with us this morning. That's all.

ETHEL. Yessir. Thank you.

> [*She goes out.* MR. GOULD *looks at his wife. When he is quite sure that she is too occupied with her handkerchief to notice him, he pulls out his own; and walking to the window, does his best to efface any signs of weakness on his part.*

MRS. GOULD. It's two hundred and forty-three days since he left here, and ever since then, every hour almost, he's been in danger... and now... he'll be standing in this room again... We must telephone to Jean—she'll come round.

MR. GOULD. Don't we... don't you... want the boy to yourself for a bit?

MRS. GOULD. He must find everything he wants when he comes home... and he'll want her... Father, if he's home long enough perhaps they can get married. I had a talk to her the other day. Dear, dear Jean—

what this'll mean to her ...' She must be here when he comes. [*She has risen to go to the telephone and notices the breakfast table.*] Dear, aren't you going to finish your breakfast ?

MR. GOULD. No. The young rascal's spoilt my appetite. Does he say what time he's coming ?

MRS. GOULD. It says this morning—that's all. [*She is at the telephone.*] Number 2147 Museum, please ... Yes, please. Father, will you send Ethel to me ? [MR. GOULD *goes out.*] Is that you, Bailey ? It's Mrs. Gould. Would you ask Miss Jean to come round here at once ? ... she started ? ... Oh ! ... Something to tell us ? ... Well, I suppose she's heard Master Harold's coming home ... she hasn't ? ... Then what *is* she coming to tell us ? ... You don't know ... yes ... well, she ought to be here now if she's been gone ten minutes ... yes, I must wait ... yes ... Good-bye, Bailey.

[*She rings off.* ETHEL *is in the room.*] I wonder what ... Margery Willis was excited too, father said ; and she's coming round ... Ethel, what's the telegram say exactly ? ... it's on the table.

ETHEL. [*Reading.*] 'With you this morning, Harold' —that's all, Mrs. Gould.

MRS. GOULD. Yes. [*She puzzles over it for a moment —then*] His room must be put ready, Ethel.

ETHEL. Yes'm, of course.

MRS. GOULD. I'd better come and see about it myself.

ETHEL. We can do everything quite well.

MRS. GOULD. I'd like to do it myself ... It seems the same as when he used to come back from school for the holidays ... getting his room ready ... it seems only the other day. I can remember the first time he ever came back from a boarding-school ... quite distinctly I can remember ... he came in at that door and ran across the room with his arms open ... to me there ... and jumped right into my arms ... and now, the things he must have been through—and he'll be standing in this room again. [*A loud ring at the bell.*] Oh, there, that's Miss Jean ... she's got something to tell me. Let her in quick.

> [ETHEL, *on her way to the door, glances out of the window and stops short.*

ETHEL. It isn't Miss Jean'm. I thought it wasn't her ring.

MRS. GOULD. Not Miss Jean ... who is it?

ETHEL. It's a soldier'm.

MRS. GOULD. Not ... not Master Harold?

ETHEL. Oh, no'm. Not him.

MRS. GOULD. Let him in, Ethel — and tell your master.

> [ETHEL *goes out and comes in again, showing in* COLONEL FANE, *a staff officer of about forty, looking very military and awe-inspiring in his smart khaki much adorned with red. He is* MRS. GOULD'S *brother.*

MRS. GOULD. Eric !

COLONEL FANE. Well, have you heard?

MRS. GOULD. We've just this minute had the wire.

COLONEL. You've had a wire?

MRS. GOULD. Yes.

COLONEL. Who from?

MRS. GOULD. Why from him—from Harold.

COLONEL. Where from?

MRS. GOULD.   From where he landed—at least I suppose so.

COLONEL.   Let's have a look.   [*She gives him the telegram.*] ... This is all you've heard?

MRS. GOULD.   All?

COLONEL.   You haven't heard anything more?

MRS. GOULD.   More? ...   Eric, there's nothing ... he's not hurt?

COLONEL.   No—he's not hurt.

MRS. GOULD.   Then what more?   What is it, Eric, what is it?

COLONEL.   Nothing but good news ... great news.

MR. GOULD *comes in.*

MR. GOULD.   Hullo, Eric!   Come round to tell us the news, eh?   You're too late, my boy.   We're before you ... just had a wire.

COLONEL.   I was just telling May there isn't everything in that wire.

MR. GOULD.   [*Collapsing.*]   Good God!   There's nothing the matter ... he's not ...

MRS. GOULD.   Now don't be silly, father!

COLONEL.   It's good news for you ... great news. You ought to be the happiest and the proudest people in England to-day ... Harold's coming back to you ... and he's coming back a hero ... recommended for gallantry ... it's a D.S.O.

> [MRS. GOULD *just sits down.* MR. GOULD *walks about. Fast. Up and down. He is shaking his head ; smiling ; sniffing violently ; and tears are streaming down his face. Presently he goes and shakes hands with the* COLONEL *; he pats his wife's arm and presses her hand in his.*

*Eventually he comes to anchor by the fireplace.
There has been a ring at the bell.*

MR. GOULD. Well ... let's ... let's hear about it.

COLONEL. He retook a section of a trench with a
few men. They say he was magnificent ... according
to them he must have accounted for several of the
enemy himself ... Fine ... magnificent ... apparently
he was missing ...

MRS. GOULD. Missing?

COLONEL. Yes—for more than twelve hours—got
back at night.

    [JEAN *enters. She is about twenty-two, and the
    eldest of a large family. Before she had really
    mastered the art of walking herself, she was pre-
    sented with an absurd wriggly little baby brother,
    whom she promptly began to look after; and
    among three subsequent arrivals she has always
    been the mother-child—loving, patient, and efficient.
    Even now, when her deep eyes are alight for her
    lover, and she is tremendously excited, there is
    over her always a beauty of soft gentleness.*

JEAN. [*A daily illustrated paper in her hand.*] Have
you seen? ... There's a picture of him.

MRS. GOULD. [*Rising.*] Jean, my dear.

JEAN. [*Going straight into Mrs. Gould's arms.*] Oh,
Mrs. Gould ...   [*The arms receive her.*

MR. GOULD. Well, well! Let's have a look. [*But
his wife does not take her arms from about the girl, and
he has to gain possession of the paper for himself, from
*JEAN'S *hand; he bears it off, and searches to find the
picture.*] Where is it? ... Eh? ... I can't see it ...
Where are my spectacles? ... I had 'em just now ...
On the table, I expect ... [*It is the* COLONEL *who finds*

them.] Now ... where are we? ... Ah! Lieutenant Gould. Yes. I shouldn't have known him from Adam.

JEAN. D'you see what it's headed?

MR. GOULD. Yes. [*Which is sandwiched between a gulp and a sniff.*]

MRS. GOULD. What is it headed, father?

MR. GOULD. It's headed ... [*But he doesn't trust himself.*] Dammit, you read it out, Jean. [*He gives his spectacles an entirely unnecessary polishing.*] Don't know what's the matter with these glasses ... can't see a dam' thing.

JEAN. [*With the words by heart.*] It says 'For Distinguished Service—Another Young Hero.'

MR. GOULD. Young scoundrel! [*He hands the paper to his wife.*] There it is, mother.

MRS. GOULD. Here's some more underneath ... It's very small print. [*She reads.*] 'Ridding the world of the Hun. Lieutenant Gould accounts for six of his country's foes. For such magnificent work this young hero is to be awarded the medal for distinguished service.'

[MR. GOULD *is looking over his wife's shoulder, and while their eyes feast upon the paper the* COLONEL *shakes hands with* JEAN.

COLONEL. May I offer my very best congratulations?

JEAN. Thanks.

COLONEL. I don't know which is to be envied most —you or he.

MRS. GOULD. [*After a great look at the paper.*] Yes. I could tell ... and he'll be standing in this room again ... Eric, do you know what time he'll be here?

COLONEL. That's one of the things I came round about ... I happened to hear what train his lot's coming up by. If we go down to the station now, we ought just about to meet it.

MRS. GOULD. [*Rising.*] Quickly ... we mustn't be late.

COLONEL. No violent hurry. Start in five minutes in a taxi.

MRS. GOULD. Will he be wearing ... IT ... his medal? [*Her voice is hushed as if she were speaking of something holy.*]

COLONEL. No, he won't ... He may not even know about it.

MR. GOULD. You mean he may get the news from us?

COLONEL. It's quite possible.

MRS. GOULD. Father, go and get ready ... Jean ...

[*But into the room like a wind comes another young lady—MARGERY WILLIS. She wears a coat and skirt of khaki, a leather belt and strap, a Colonial slouch hat—it is some kind of uniform. She has made herself as much like the military as possible, and at once takes command.*

MARGERY WILLIS. [*She too has the illustrated paper.*] I say, you people—congrats—have you seen? Oh, yes, you've got it—d'you see what it says—SIX of 'em. By Jove, wish I'd seen it ... it must have been GREAT. I say, Mrs. Gould, you must be tremendously proud. [*She kisses her; to the COLONEL :*] How d'... [*But she remembers just in time and, drawing herself up, salutes.*] I say, congrats, Mr. Gould ... and Jean ... I say, Jean, it must be rather wonderful for you. Fancy being loved by a hero.

JEAN. Yes.

MARGERY. [*Holding out her hand.*] It's awfully difficult to say what you mean, you know, but ... well, by Jove, congrats. [*Instead of shaking hands she kisses* JEAN.] When's he going to be here? We all want to come in and cheer.

MRS. GOULD. We're going down to meet him now.

MARGERY. By Jove!—wish we could come... can't spare the time, though... we got a terrific day. Making munitions all the morning... giving a concert—you know, Pierrot show; I'm going to sing 'The Arms of the Army'—hot stuff, I can tell you—with Jack as the chorus; he does look an ass doing it. There'll be a whole heap of Tommies there, and this evening the Rector's making up a party, and we're all going to the Royal Opera House to hear St. John Bullock on 'War —the new Religion.' He's FINE. Dad used to call him the biggest scoundrel unhung before the war—but it's wonderful how it's brought all classes and people together, isn't it?... The old Bish is in the chair... Well, so long... I must go. They're waiting outside. I say, Jean, you should come along and munish... it's terrific sport making shells... wish I could be at the station to cheer—we'll all look in some time to-day, though, you bet... So long... *Six* of 'em.

[*She goes out.*

MRS. GOULD. Come along, father, and get your things on... Eric, will you get a taxi for us?

COLONEL. Certainly.

[*He and* MR. GOULD *go out; as* MRS. GOULD *is going* JEAN'S *voice stops her.*

JEAN. Mrs. Gould.

MRS. GOULD. Yes, dear?

JEAN. I don't think I shall come down to the station.

MRS. GOULD. Not come?

JEAN. No, I'd rather not. Somehow, I... I don't

want to meet him with all the other people about. I don't think I could bear it... Will you tell him I'm waiting here for him... May I? I'd rather.

MRS. GOULD. Of course you shall.

JEAN. [*With a quaint little twinkle.*] Don't kiss me. I should start crying.

MRS. GOULD. I know... I'll bring him straight back to you.

JEAN. Thank you.

> [MRS. GOULD *goes out.* JEAN *has not been alone for a moment when* ETHEL *comes in to clear away the breakfast things.*

ETHEL. Oh, I beg your pardon, Miss Jean... I thought you was gone.

JEAN. Come in, Ethel.

ETHEL. Shall I be in your way if I clears, Miss?

JEAN. Not a bit.

> [ETHEL *begins to clear; then presently:*

ETHEL. It's fine about Mr. Harold, isn't it?

JEAN. Yes.

ETHEL. Must be all right for you... wish it was my Tom.

JEAN. I didn't know you had any one out there, Ethel.

ETHEL. Near twelve months 'e's been out there... my Tom 'as.

JEAN. Is he your...

ETHEL. Yes. My young man... near twelve months I ain't seen 'im. [*Her thoughts find words in spasmodic sentences as she busies herself with the breakfast things.*] ... twelve months come next Friday week... I could do without the 'ero part to get him back for a bit... just for an evening out with 'im... a sweetheart, two brothers an' a father at it ... I've given my bit to 'em ... seems crool, don't it ?... all for you-don't-know-what like.

JEAN. They're fighting for you, Ethel, and for me, and for their country.

ETHEL. [*A little unresponsive to this—her thoughts are travelling along their own lines.*] Yes ... *any'ow*, now they *'ave* gorn, them wot stays be'ind don't 'arf make me *wild* ... the shirkers don't ... 'oldin' meetin's, some of 'em ... *I'd* give 'em shirkers ... you should 'ear my brother Bert ... 'e's a corporal.

JEAN. [*With a big enthusiasm and sincerity, though her voice never loses its gentleness.*] Yes—it's a great war for freedom and liberty.

ETHEL. [*Again her thoughts have pursued their own way.*] ... Broke up one of their meetin's, 'e did ... 'e and the boys.

JEAN. Oh! What was it about?

ETHEL. They didn't know rightly what it was *about* —something they didn't like ... *any'ow*, there wasn't much more of it after they got in ... Australians, they are ... the boys ... Bert's friends ... fine big fellars... there was a young chap on the platform makin' a speech or somethink ... they pulled 'im orf ... and 'is glasses fell orf 'an 'e trod on 'em 'isself ... LARF !!!! I thought I should er died.

> [*She disappears with the loaded tray. Back again, she folds up the table-cloth and puts it away in a drawer. From where she is she can see out of the window.*

ETHEL. There they go.

JEAN. [*Hurrying to the window and waving from it.*] How long d'you think they'll be, Ethel?

ETHEL. Ought to be back in the 'arf-hour ... and

then Mr. Harold 'll be here . . . Coo! If it were my Tom.

[JEAN *watches her as she stands staring in front of her, picturing to herself his home-coming. There is a queer little smile on her lips, a tightening in her throat, and tears are filling into her eyes that do not see what they are looking at. Her voice is uncertain of itself.*

It'll be funny—'im coming back again . . . you can't seem to fancy some'ow . . . it don't seem as if it 'ud ever really *'appen*—'im coming back again . . . near twelve months it's been just thinkin' of 'im all the time— all the time it 'as . . . and . . . Oh, *you* know, wantin' 'im.

[*The little smile twists itself all wrong; the tears well up, and her longing finds expression as best it may.*

Oh, I *do* wish it were 'im coming.

JEAN. [*Touched and sympathetic and feeling a little helpless.*] Ethel, so do I . . . I wish it were him coming too.

[JEAN'S *voice recalls the girl back to the room again. She shuts her eyes very tight to squeeze them dry, she bites her lip very hard to get the smile back into shape—and she wins.*

ETHEL. . . . But 'e ain't — and that's all there is about it.

[*She goes to the door. Two large tears have over-flowed and tremble, like two large raindrops, on the brinks of her cheeks—the only tokens of the recent storm.*

Is there anything you want, Miss Jean ?

JEAN. No, thank you, Ethel. [ETHEL *turns to go, but* JEAN *feels that she does want to try and say some-*

thing.] Oh, Ethel... [ETHEL *faces round again—and*
JEAN *hesitates for words.*] I ...

ETHEL. Don't say anything about *'im*, please, Miss.

JEAN. I don't want anything, thank you.

ETHEL. Thank you, Miss.

> [*And she goes out.* JEAN *selects a book and sits by
> the fireplace—her back to the door—half reading,
> half dreaming. After a little while of silence,
> the door opens quietly, and* HAROLD, *in civilian
> clothes, is standing in the room. The girl has not
> heard him come in, and realising that if he spoke
> he would startle her, he stands there, behind her,
> hesitating and uncertain. At last he speaks, very
> softly.*

HAROLD. Jeanie!

> [JEAN *looks quickly up, but does not turn her head.
> She thinks her ears are playing her strange tricks,
> as they have done before in the night silences.
> For a moment she listens, and then, sinking her
> head between her hands, covers her ears as if she
> would shut out the sound.* HAROLD *waits where
> he is. Then, when her ears are free again, a
> little stronger :*

It's all right, Jeanie ; it's me ...

> [*She rises and faces him, too utterly surprised to do
> anything for the moment but stare at him.*

... Hullo !... [*His eyes wander vaguely round the
room ; his voice, as vaguely, seems to echo his thoughts.*]
... They've moved the piano... it used to be over
there.

JEAN. But I don't understand... how have you got
here—and like that ?

HAROLD. There was a fuss down there at the station

D

... and I left them ... I oughtn't to have done ... and come up in a taxi ... where's everybody? ... where's mother?

JEAN. They've gone down to the station to meet you.

HAROLD. [*Repeating himself.*] There was a fuss ... I came up in a taxi ... and went up to my room ... why have they taken the big picture of me down from over my bed?

JEAN. It's in your mother's room.

HAROLD. Oh! ... I changed my things ... I didn't want you to see me in them ...

JEAN. Not want me to see you in them! Why, Harold! Harold, you stupid ...

[*She advances towards him, ready to move close into his arms and take him back to her—if he had opened them to receive her. But he does not. And as, closer to him now, she looks into his eyes, something in them begins to frighten her.*]

This isn't a bit like I expected ... your coming home ... not a bit.

HAROLD. Look at me. [*It is a command.*] Look straight at me.

JEAN. Harold!

HAROLD. You *are* like her ...

JEAN. Harold!

HAROLD. [*With an indicating movement of his hand across his own forehead.*] All across there you are ... and your hair ... the wavy bit.

JEAN. Harold ... dear ... what are you talking about?

HAROLD. ... and your eyes are terribly like ... [*He looks suddenly over his shoulder, and then apprehensively round the room.*] ... do you think people haunt you?

[*By this time* JEAN, *realising that he is almost unconscious of her, feeling that there is something
between them through which she cannot reach
him, can only stand watching him, hypnotised, as
it were, by his fearful strangeness.*

No; of course they don't ... Of course they don't. I
don't believe in ghosts. There isn't anything any more
after you've been killed ... Only, if there is, would they
go on haunting you for the rest of your life ... there
can't be anything after you're dead ... there are so
many of them ... and yet [*a great fear comes into his
voice*] he spoke to me on the boat ... I heard his voice.

[*He has said that so directly to her, that she answers.*
JEAN. Whose voice ? ... I don't understand.
HAROLD. He's dead now ... and he had a locket-
thing ... and she was like you; and on the boat at
night, when it was all dark, he came and asked for it ...
and I gave it to him ... and he took it away ... Of
course, it may have just fallen into the sea ... I was
leaning over ... and I stretched out my hand with it ...
only I heard his voice, just as if you'd spoken to me ...
suppose I was to hear it again now [*he is as terrified
as a child*] and I've given him back his locket ... I can't
do anything more, can I ? ...

[*He has gone to her as if for protection.*
JEAN. [*Quieting him as she might one of her young
brothers.*] There ... my dear ... there isn't anything to
be frightened of ... if you'd only tell me ... what is it
that's between us ... I don't understand in the least
what you're talking about. I want to help. Won't you
tell me quite quietly ?

HAROLD. It's all muddled—the beginning ... out of
our trench into theirs ... where *they* were ... and men

coming at you ... their faces quite close ... and shoot-
ing at them ... and the hellish noise and the shouting
... and our men with bayonets... and somebody
screamed ... it went right into him ... and then ... *him.*

[*He pauses as if trying to recall the details to his
mind.* JEAN *waits. He begins again in a low,
dull monotone.*]

He was just a grey thing at first coming at me ... I
hadn't got a shot left and I hit at him, with something
in my hand ... a sort of knife ... into his face ... into
his mouth ... against his teeth ... and my hand came
out with a lot of blood and things ... I remember
thinking how I used to hate going to the dentist when I
was a kid ... I remember thinking that, quite distinctly
... and while I was thinking of the time I had a tooth
out ... this big one at the back ... we got clutched up
together ... then we fell ... I was right on top of him,
and the thing I had in my hand—it must have been a
knife—it went right into his stomach ... right in ... I
fell on him ...... then I was lying on top of him, and
I looked at him ; quite still he was ... I looked quite a
long time ... I looked at his face ... he was just about
my age ... and I put my hand over the part that was
all smashed, and I thought how good-looking he was ...
hair with the tiniest little curls, *you* know ... then I
raised myself up and took the knife out ... it had gone
right in him, and then all sideways ... and I tried to
undo his tunic, but it was all—Oh, I didn't do it! you
see, I'd fallen on him ; it wasn't my fault exactly ...
and then he began to cry out ... and I knew it must be
hurting him simply horribly ... he kept on crying out
—and he wouldn't stop ... Oh, it was too awful! and I
tried to kill him.   [*A movement, at last, from* JEAN.

It was the only thing, to put an end to it ... but I couldn't ... till I put my fingers round his throat and pressed ... and I pressed and I pressed ... he couldn't struggle much ... I watched the life die out of his eyes ...

[*His low voice drops into silence; after a little his recollection of it again becomes audible.*]

... like something going a long way away behind a glass ... and just before it went out altogether, he put up his hand to his neck ... not to try and take my fingers away ... but his fingers undid a button ... there wasn't any sight left in his eyes ... and the locket was there ... his fingers clenched round it, and I thought it was all over and let go with my hands ... and suddenly, quite beautifully and low, he spoke a girl's name ... and the pain all went out of his eyes, and he looked, like you look sometimes, loving and longing and hopeful ... I opened it, and I thought I was looking at you, and I realised it was *his* you ... and he's out there thrown in somewhere with a heap of others, with some earth scrambled over them ... and she's there waiting ... do you think he came back and took it away, or do you think I just dropped it into the sea?

JEAN. [*Caressing him with her voice.*] My dear, my dear, it isn't your fault; you didn't want the war; nobody in England wanted the war—we're fighting in self-defence.

HAROLD. [*Looking quickly up at her; he is evidently making a great effort at concentration—his voice is more certain of itself, more argumentative.*] Look here, Jean ... I've been thinking—I've been thinking quite a lot ...

ETHEL *comes in, white and dishevelled.*

ETHEL. Miss Jean. May I speak to you, please,

Miss. [*She sees that* JEAN *is not alone.*] Oh, I beg your pardon ... I thought ...

JEAN. [*Noticing her face.*] Ethel, what is it?

ETHEL. I thought you were alone.

JEAN. Whatever is it, Ethel? What's the matter?

ETHEL. I come to you, Miss. I just seen it in the lists ... 'e won't never come 'ome to me now.

JEAN. Tom?

ETHEL. Killed, it said.

JEAN. [*Going to her.*] Oh, my dear.

ETHEL. I just seen it ... just this minute ... I can't seem to think ... I shan't never see 'im no more ... an' I shan't never marry 'im—an' I shan't never love 'im proper ... an' I 'ope them wot killed 'im is dead themselves by now.

HAROLD. Don't say things like that, Ethel ... they've all got homes of their own—and lovers ...

ETHEL. Them! *'Uns!!* They're not worth nothink —Oh, I wish I was a man—you done your bit fine, Mr. Harold ... You've killed 'em—the devils ... six of 'em ...

JEAN. [*Trying to keep these last words from his ears.*] Ethel!

ETHEL. I'm sorry, Miss ... I come to you ... but I thought you was alone. [*She turns to go.*

JEAN. Don't go.

ETHEL. Yes, I want to ... up to my room, alone ... you've got yours back, and I shan't never ... I wish black 'Ell to them wot killed 'im, and if there's any justice in 'Eaven, God'll give it to 'em.

[*She breaks down utterly, and finds her way from the room, sobbing terribly.*

JEAN. How dreadful—poor, poor Ethel.

HAROLD. That's how it goes on ... there are people over there cursing me like that. [*He seems to lose grip of the present again, and his thoughts turn inwards.*] If only I knew what his name was, and where he lived ... and where she lives ... I thought I might ... I might go over and see her ... d'you think I could ... after the war? ... I could tell her it wasn't my fault—you see, it wasn't; I fell on him ... [*Then, quite suddenly :*] How did she know about it? How did that girl know? ... [JEAN *has no answer.*] ... Do you know how she knew? ...

JEAN. [*Very low.*] No ... I don't know.

HAROLD. It's between him and me ... something I've got to make up for, if I can ... nobody else must know ever ... only just you ... I had to tell some one. I shan't even tell mother and dad ... you won't tell them, will you? ... [*Again* JEAN *is silent.*] ... you won't?

JEAN. [*As low as before.*] No.

HAROLD. Only just you and I know and *him* ... but she knew ... she said something about six ... what did she mean? ... Jean, what *did* she mean? [*The idea flashes on him.*] It's not in the newspapers ... not for everybody to know ... My God! I couldn't bear it if it was—I should go mad.

JEAN. You mustn't say things like that ... and you mustn't worry.

HAROLD. Is it in the papers?

JEAN. My dear ... why should it be?

HAROLD. Is it?

JEAN. No.

[*The Illustrated Daily Paper has been lying open on the table;* JEAN *folds it up and removes it as unobtrusively as she can.*

HAROLD. If it had been ... I don't know what I should
have done ... I don't *know* what I should have done.

[*The door opens and* MR. GOULD *stands on the
threshold. It is to be noticed that he is carrying
the illustrated paper. As* JEAN *turns to the
sound of the opening door, she happens to hide*
HAROLD.

MR. GOULD. [*Speaking at once.*] I say, Jean, my
dear, you mustn't be disappointed ... there's a mystery
—nothing to alarm you ... We met the train, but he
hasn't c—— [*and he sees* HAROLD. *His mouth is open to
complete the word, and it just stays open.*] Why, God
bless my soul, here he is. [*He dashes at him.*] My dear
old chap!

[*He grips his hand, nearly shakes his arm off, and
kisses him.* COLONEL FANE *has appeared in the
doorway.*

I say, Eric, here he is. God knows how he got here;
but here he is. Tell his mother. No, I will.

[*He returns to the open door—calling—evidently far
too excited to know what he is doing.*

Mother! ... Mother! ... Where are you? ... MOTHER!

MRS. GOULD'S VOICE. [*As she is coming downstairs.*]
Yes, dear?

MR. GOULD. I've got a little surprise for you ...
come along ... a little unbirthday present.

MRS. GOULD. [*Appearing.*] What is it, dear?

Mr. GOULD. [*His hand outstretched to Harold.*] There
... look what I've got for you ... found it lying about
when I came in.

MRS. GOULD. Boy!

HAROLD. Hullo, mother!

[*She takes him to her with an enormous kiss.*

MR. GOULD. What *I* want to know is—what's he doing here? Did he fly in through the window, Jean?

JEAN. He came up by himself in a taxi.

MR. GOULD. Oh! [*He eyes him proudly, still in his mother's embrace.*] Got into his own things, too... Well, you've had the first look at him... You've told him the news?

JEAN. No.

MR. GOULD. You haven't?

JEAN. No.

MR. GOULD. [*Waving the paper.*] You haven't shown him this?

JEAN. No.

MR. GOULD. [*Thrusting the paper into her hands.*] Well, then, show it to him now.

JEAN. Oh, no, Mr. Gould—please.

MR. GOULD. Yes, my dear. You're the right person to do it... I don't say I don't envy you.

HAROLD. [*Whose attention has been caught.*] What is it?

MR. GOULD. Jean's got something in the paper to show you.

[*He urges the unwilling girl so that she stands right before* HAROLD.

JEAN. [*Helpless.*] Mr. Gould!

HAROLD. [*Quickly.*] Something about me?

MR. GOULD. Yes.

HAROLD. Something in the paper about me?

MR. GOULD. Yes... Come along, Jean.

JEAN. I'd rather not, really; not now.

MR. GOULD. Eh?

HAROLD. Show it to me. [*She puts the paper into*

his hands. He scans the sheet.] ... I don't see anything
... what is it?... Where?

MR. GOULD.   You've given him the wrong side of it
now. 'Pon my word, I believe you're frightened it'll
turn his head! [HAROLD *reverses the paper.*] The top
picture on the left... and, by Jove! old chap, we're
proud of you... we are... we're proud... eh?

>   [HAROLD *has looked up, and the sentence ends with a
>   little noise in his throat.*

HAROLD. [*Almost to himself.*] No... it isn't true
... it isn't true. [*He stares at the little group; and,
hypnotised as* JEAN *was, they wait in silence. He is
evidently striving again with the past.*] ... There were
six in it when I started, and it was empty when *he*
came... if I could remember... O, my Christ! if it *is*
true... and they want to reward me for it. [*He talks
horribly in the air.*] I won't take it... I won't touch
it... you *know* I won't, don't you? [*He sinks into a
chair, covering his face with his hands.*] O, my Christ!

MR. GOULD. Hullo!

MRS. GOULD. What is it?

JEAN. He's been telling me—it isn't a bit like we
expected... he's been telling me about the man he
killed.

COLONEL. It's all right, people; they're often like
that at first... shock, you know—nerves... he'll be all
right in a day or two.

>   [HAROLD *has not raised his head from his hands,
>   and* MR. GOULD, *going to him, pats him gently
>   and kindly on the shoulder.*

MR. GOULD. There, there, there, my dear old chap;
we understand... of course, we do... one or two good
breakfasts at home, a few nights in your own comfort-

able bed, and a dinner with me at the Club, eh?...
you'll be as right as rain. [*No answer.*] Come along,
old man, pull yourself together. [*No answer.*] It sounds
strange, here in my own house, telling the soldier who's
been facing death for us for nearly a year to ' pull himself together.'

HAROLD. [*Suddenly looking up.*] It isn't a soldier's
job to get killed ... it's his job to kill.

MR. GOULD. [*Momentarily nonplussed.*] Yes ... but—

HAROLD. You know, it isn't *them* so much ... or
even *him* ... it's her, waiting there ... coming back to
Jean makes you realise.

MR. GOULD. Oh, come, come, come!... you've killed
your men, we know ; but it was in fair fight.

HAROLD. Fair fight!

MR. GOULD. Well, if it wasn't fair fight, it wasn't *you*
that was fighting foul ... we know *that* ... I shouldn't
let myself be weak.

HAROLD. Fair fight! If you only knew what it
means ... all of it ... all fighting's foul!

MR. GOULD. Oh, come—that's rather a queer view!
[*He tries a little joviality.*] We get quite enough of that
sort of thing from the cranks at home. We can't do
with any sentimentalism, you know, from the men who
are doing the work.

HAROLD. Fair fight!

[*He is evidently on the verge of breaking down completely. THE COLONEL, who is not a man of words,
has taken up his position with his back to the
fireplace ; MRS. GOULD and JEAN can only watch
and listen. When MR. GOULD speaks again, he
is entirely serious.*

MR. GOULD. Come, old man, I want you to listen

to me, quietly... are you listening? [HAROLD *nods assent.*] ... Look here... if a criminal was to come into this room and attack me, or your mother, or Jean, you'd be the first to protect us... Eh?... of course you would. Well, that's what you've been doing... and you wouldn't be so much upset if you happened to damage the blackguard in the process... of course you wouldn't ... my dear old chap, nobody wanted this war... but if you're attacked you've got to defend yourself... That's all it is... it's perfectly simple... but, by Jove! we *are* proud of you, and we *are* thankful to you for the way you've been protecting your home, and your country, and all that she stands for.

HAROLD. D'you know when I heard all that last? ... all of it almost... in their trenches. [*He has risen in a passionate, nervous excitement.*] I was lying there all night, quite close, and I heard them talking, just like our chaps do sometimes—laughing and joking about all the things they're going through, and knowing they've got to climb out in the morning and don't stand a dog's chance of being alive—not death itself simply, but bits of you smashed up, and you lie and roll about; you can hear them crying out all over the place—and the night before they wait... and make fun... and they know all the time—it's just in the early morning, when it gets a bit colder and the light begins to come in the sky, waiting—my God! they are fine, all of 'em... d'you think they'd do that to each other, month after month, if they didn't both think they were right and the others wrong, and they were protecting something? It's all a bloody muddle!

MR. GOULD. Harold!!

HAROLD. It is!!!... If you'd heard them. There

was a man there—a Socialist or something, I suppose—
talking against the war... and the way they all sat on
him. They got furious with him. They talked just like
you... how they were afraid of Russia and France and
England all against them, and how nobody wanted the
war; and how, now it had come, they must all protect
their wives and their children, and their homes and their
country... and they told each other stories to prove
what brutes we were... stories of what the Russians
had done... filthy things... and the French foreign
troops... I don't know if they were true, but they were
just the same as we say about them... [THE COLONEL
and MR. GOULD *begin to get restive. They would inter-
rupt, but in his growing passion he gives them no oppor-
tunity.*] ... Who makes everybody believe it's somebody
else's fault? They believe it... *you* believe it... Jean
said it to me... There were two men in our company
from the dirty little street out at the back there... what
have I ever done for them before the war?

MR. GOULD. [*Getting a word in.*] Really! That's
got nothing to do with it—you're only worrying
yourself.

HAROLD. [*Turning on him.*] It *has* got something
to do with it... I want Jean to understand, and mother,
and you, and all decent people... [*He tries to put into
words an idea he has been worrying at.*] I mean, what
have you, or any one in this whole street of great big
houses, ever really done about the beastly little streets
just behind at our back-doors... a whole wilderness,
miles and miles of 'em... except pretend they aren't
there?... and it's the same in other countries... It's
their job to join together and get a more decent share
of life, instead of being born and living and dying

in ugliness... only we put expensive weapons into their hands, and tell them to go and kill one another. And they do. That's the horrible part. They do. We put 'em in uniforms, and yell 'Form fours! as you were!' at 'em, till they'll do *anything*. They're tremendously brave—they're magnificent. I know, I've seen 'em—but the waste! [THE COLONEL *makes a short advance from his position on the hearthrug, clears his throat, and is, unfortunately, at once overwhelmed.*] After all, what's it matter who was to blame in the beginning! It's happened. And all the young men in the world, and the workpeople who didn't have anything to do with starting it—and all think they're right—are tearing one another to pieces in screaming agony... It ought to be stopped... aren't there enough sane people in the world to prevent it ever happening again... now they've seen what it's like?... If only they'd find a way of stopping it!... D'you know what I thought the other day?—if we could get some of the statesmen, and the newspaper men, and the parsons, and the clever writers in all the countries who keep it going—put them in a room—with knives—sharp knives —and let them hurt one another—hurt one another horribly—stick them in, and scream with pain... or, with a few bombs—and their legs and arms and hands and feet just torn off... great gashing holes in them ... My God, they'd want to stop soon enough—they'd 'start negotiations' all right—only now they just sit at home, the old men, and set us at each other.

MR. GOULD. [*Feeling he is being implicated.*] This is monstrous!

HAROLD. [*The anger in his father's tone rousing its answer in his.*] You sent me out there, and I've done the life out of a man my own age... He looked a ripping good sort, and I might have liked him, and you want to reward me for it ... and if he'd have killed me—he might just as well, only I fell on him—you and Jean and all of you'd have been miserable—and they'd have rewarded him ... it's all so dam' *silly*.

COLONEL. The best thing you can do is to lie down for a bit ... I must get back to the War Office.

HAROLD. [*Going straight on.*] Dam' silly ... I saw as I came up from the station, 'No Peace Piffle' on the 'buses ... and a whole lot of men learning to prod sacks with bayonets ... and they were laughing—God in Heaven, I used to laugh.

MARGERY WILLIS *bursts in.*

MARGERY. Has he come? [*She sees him.*] There he is! Three cheers for Lieutenant Gould, D.S.O. [*She calls out of the door :*] I say, you people, he's here. Come along up and cheer ... I'll bring 'em in. [*She disappears calling :*] Jack, Audrey, Daddy—he's here ... Come on in ...

COLONEL. [*Feeling that these things should not be heard outside.*] I don't think I should say any more now, if I were you; at least—don't. You mustn't say anything more now. You must be quiet.

HAROLD. It's no use ordering me about, because I've done with it. Oh, I know, I know. You all think I'm mad—looking at me like that. [*He has completely lost control of himself; his words rush out in an ever-growing crescendo.*] But there are millions doing it—millions. The young ones doing it, and the old ones feeling noble about it ... Yes, Dad feels noble because I've killed somebody ... I saw him feeling noble ... and you all look at me, because I tell you it's all filthy ... foul

language and foul thinking and stinking bits of bodies
all about ... millions at it ... it's not me that's mad ...
it's the whole world that's mad ...   I've done with it ...
I've done with it ...   That man in their trenches—he'd
had enough ... he said he was going to refuse to kill
any more, and they called him traitor and pro-English,
and they've probably shot him by now ...   Well, you
can shoot me ... because I'm not going back ... I'm
going to stop at home and say it's all mad ... I'm going
to keep on saying it ... somebody's got to stop some-
time ... somebody's got to get sane again ... and I
won't go back ... I won't, I won't ... I won't ...

MARGERY. [*In the doorway, cheering wildly.*] HUR-
RAY, HURRAY. [*There are sounds and voices in the
passage: ' Where is he?'—' He's in the dining-room'—
' Come along in '—' Three cheers for Harold.'*] HIP, HIP,
HURRAY ... HIP, HIP, HURRAY ... HIP, HIP, HURRAY !

   [*But as he stands there, white, with clenched fists,
      and still, the* CURTAIN *comes quickly down and
      hides him.*

THE END.

Printed in the United States
114289LV00007B/168/A